better together*

* This book is best read together, grownup and kid.

a **akidsco.com**

a
kids
book
about

a kids book about Addiction.

by Nicole Lendo

A Kids Co.
Editor Denise Morales Soto
Designer Rick DeLucco
Creative Director Rick DeLucco
Studio Manager Kenya Feldes
Sales Director Melanie Wilkins
Head of Books Jennifer Goldstein
CEO and Founder Jelani Memory

DK
Delhi Technical Team Bimlesh Tiwary Pushpak Tyagi, Rakesh Kumar
Senior Production Editor Jennifer Murray
Senior Production Controller Louise Minihane
Senior Acquisitions Editor Katy Flint
Acquisitions Project Editor Sara Forster
Managing Art Editor Vicky Short
Managing Director, Licensing Mark Searle

First American edition, 2025
Published in the United States by DK Publishing, 1745 Broadway, 20th Floor,
New York, NY 10019

First published in Great Britain in 2025 by
Dorling Kindersley Limited, 20 Vauxhall Bridge Road, London SW1V 2SA
A Penguin Random House Company

The authorised representative in the EEA is
Dorling Kindersley Verlag GmbH. Arnulfstr. 124, 80636 Munich, Germany

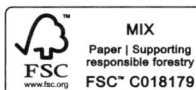

A catalog record for this book is available from the Library of Congress.
A CIP catalogue record for this book is available from the British Library.
ISBN: 978-0-2417-4393-5

DK books are available at special discounts when purchased in bulk for sales
promotions, premiums, fund-raising, or education use. For details, contact:
DK Publishing Special Markets, 1745 Broadway, 20th Floor, New York, NY 10019
SpecialSales@dk.com

Printed and bound in China
www.dk.com
akidsco.com

MIX
Paper | Supporting
responsible forestry
FSC™ C018179

This book was made with Forest
Stewardship Council™ certified
paper – one small step in DK's
commitment to a sustainable future.
**Learn more at www.dk.com/uk/
information/sustainability**

This book is dedicated to A.J., the strongest person I know.

Intro
for grownups

I want to congratulate you for picking up this book. Addiction is an extremely uncomfortable and often painful topic to think about, let alone share and discuss. But addiction is something that doesn't discriminate. It is so widespread and all-consuming, and unfortunately affects anyone and everyone who crosses its path—including kids.

Opening this door and allowing yourself and your kid to explore the impacts of addiction, as well as the reasons behind it, will validate their experience while also decreasing the stigma surrounding addiction.

Use this book to explore and understand the loop of addiction, and lessen the impact of its blows.

What is
addiction?

An addiction is when someone wants or needs something so badly that they will do anything to get it.

People who live with an addiction are often called addicts.*

*You can also say "a person who suffers with an addiction."

A person can be addicted
to a lot of things, like

drugs,

alcohol,

shopping,

eating,

gambling,

video games,

or just about anything.

But how does a person become an addict?

Well, that's a complicated answer.

First of all,
they don't choose to be one.

It's something that has always
been inside them, but one day,
without them knowing it,
it accidentally gets triggered.

A lot of things can trigger
that addiction.

Sometimes people try things not knowing that they will become addicted.

Sometimes people get hurt and doctors give them medicine to help them feel better and they end up becoming addicted to it.

Sometimes people become addicted when they try things to make them feel good.

Sometimes people don't even realize what they are doing is addictive.

How an addiction works
has to do with how the person's
brain makes connections with what
they do and see.

The brain of someone who suffers with an addiction doesn't work the same way as someone who doesn't have an addiction.

Our brains go through many steps when we do, see, and experience things. These steps are memory, motivation, reward, and control.

For example: Maybe you really like cookies. They're a special treat for you and your brain remembers that. It also remembers how great you feel after you eat a cookie and so it motivates you to get more cookies, so you keep feeling happy. But your brain also knows that eating too many cookies is bad for you, so it reminds you that you shouldn't eat all the cookies. Maybe just 1 or 2 and save the rest for another day.

If someone has an addiction, instead of going through all of these steps, their brain skips the last one (control) and creates a constant loop.

The second the substance reaches their brain for the first time...

Boom.

The loop begins.

The brain wants more.

The loop drives the addiction.

It's very difficult to escape this loop.

Actually, once the loop
has been activated, you
can never fully turn it off.

You just have to learn
to be aware of the loop
and work against it.

Still confused?

Let me explain.

Picture a flashing
red light in your
peripheral vision.

Something you can
only see out of the
corner of your eye.

You can sit up straight,
keep your eyes forward,
and stay focused,
but no matter how much
you try to ignore it or pretend
it's not there, you can still see
the red light flashing.

Taunting you, trying to get you
to look at it and lose your focus.

Always.

Red. Re

ed. Red.

When someone's addiction is triggered, it becomes their whole world.

Addicts may do anything to get the thing that they are addicted to.

Anything.

Even if it's bad for them.
Even if it hurts other people.

They don't mean
to hurt other people.

A lot of the time they don't
even realize they're doing it.

They are living in the loop
and can't see anything outside of it.

They can't see how they are
affecting everyone around them.

Sometimes they don't even
realize they're in the loop at all.

If someone you know or love is in that loop of addiction, it can be a difficult thing to cope* with.

*To cope means to deal with or overcome problems or situations.

You might feel lonely.

You might feel disposable.

You might feel neglected.

You might feel angry.

Frustrated.

Guilty.

Or even heartbroken.

It's OK to feel this way.

It's normal.

But you need to understand,
they aren't hurting you on purpose.

An addict is a sick person,
not a bad person.

So what they do
because of their addiction
has nothing to do with you
or anything you've done.

I promise.

The addict loves you even if they don't always show it.

They're just in the loop and you are outside of the loop.

I was outside of the loop, too.

I know how it feels to watch
someone you love struggle
with their addiction.

You feel helpless.

You feel lost and confused.

It hurts so much it feels
like you can't breathe.

Dealing with addiction never gets easier, but here are a few things you should always remember.

1.
You didn't cause the person to be an addict.

It isn't your fault.

Even if you had a temper tantrum,
even if you called them names,
even if you weren't very nice.

These things don't cause addiction.

2.

You can't control it.

Read that again—
you can't control it.

Nothing you do or don't do will
make the addict better or worse.

3.

You can't cure them.

That means there is no medicine that you can give an addict to make them better.

They must decide to get better themselves and work really hard— really, really, really hard—each and every day, to stay that way.

The road to recovery* isn't simple.

Relapse*

is common but definitely not
the end of the road.

*Recovery is the process of fighting against
 your addiction in order to get better.

*Relapse is when the addict falls back into the loop
 of addiction after they've started their recovery.

But while you can't fix someone's addiction, you can support them in their recovery.

You can tell them that you love them.

Write them letters.

Draw pictures for them.

Go on walks with them.

Give them hugs.

But always remember—

you're the kid.

The only person you need
to take care of is yourself.

You are not in charge of
someone else's recovery.

Sometimes it might
feel like you are, but that's
not your responsibility.

Sometimes it might seem like you're all you've got,

but you are strong.

You are resilient.

You are loved, even when it doesn't feel like it.

You must never forget...

Be kind to yourself.

Love yourself.

And keep moving forward.

You are doing

the best

you can,

and that's good enough.

Outro
for grownups

Whew. That was a lot. But you did it! You opened the door to discuss addiction—now what? There are a few steps you can take to make sure the kid in your life is coping with the impact that someone's addiction may have had on them.

First, if someone they know suffers from addiction, reinforce the idea that it isn't the kid's fault (and remember that it wasn't your fault either). Second, discuss healthy ways to support the addict, without enabling their addiction. Third, come up with ways to support each other, because it's just as important to take care of yourself. Fourth, talk about it. Keep talking about it. Normalize the discussion around addiction and the impact it has on your life. Talk about how it makes you feel. Talk about the feelings of isolation and shame.

Addiction doesn't need to be a dirty secret, and acknowledging that it's a part of your life is the first step toward healing.

About The Author

Nicole Lendo (she/her) has been a teacher for the past 15 years, spending the majority of her days with 7-to-11-year-olds. She fosters a strong classroom community that is built on trust, respect, and most importantly, she creates a safe space for her students.

She learned at an early age what addiction was and the impact it can have on a family. Nicole could have used a book like this as a kid.

She believes this book is a good tool for both kids and grownups to use as they navigate this difficult topic. And she hopes her readers know the symptoms of addiction are not their fault and that they can feel empowered to talk about it.

@misslendo

Made to empower.

a kids book about **racism** by Jelani Memory	a kids book about ANXIETY by Ross Szabo	a kids book about DISABILITY by Kristine Napper	a kids book about IMAGINATION by LEVAR BURTON	a kids book about *belonging* by Kevin Carroll
a kids book about failure by Dr. Laymon Hicks	a kids book about GRATITUDE by Ben Kenyon	a kids book about LIFE ONLINE by Dave S. Anderson & Blake Fleischacker	a kids book about body image by Rebecca Alexander	a kids book about IMMIGRATION by MJ Calderon
a kids book about EMPATHY by Daron K. Roberts	a kids book about GENDER by Dale Mueller	a kids book about Love by ZIGGY MARLEY	a kids book about EQUALITY by BILLIE JEAN KING	a kids book about MONEY by Adam Stramwasser
a kids book about FEMINISM by Emma McIlroy	a kids book about *adventure* by Dr. Ben Tertin	a kids book about CLIMATE CHANGE by Zanagee Artis & Olivia Greenspan	a kids book about CONFIDENCE by Joy Cho	a kids book about BEING NONBINARY by Hunter Chinn-Raicht